The North Winds Blow

The North Winds Blow

a collection of poetry

Peter Cunliffe

First Published in 2022 by Kindle | Direct Publishing

ISBN: 9798813641664

For Rosemary,
Richard, Jonathan and Joshua-James

The north winds blow

Contents

Contents

Contents

Preface and Acknowledgements

Deeply held emotion, and conflicts between faith and lived experience can be ignored or buried deep in the psyche or wrestled with to find expression in words or art. Coming from a family of artists and engineers creativity found its expression across the years and continues to burst out through the younger generations.

Scraps of paper containing the writing of my great uncle, sitting dormant in my desk, came to my attention as we commemorated the centenary years of the First World War. Those papers, written by a young man days before his mortal life ended on the fields of France, and walking those same fields 100 years later, gave an inner connection with him. They provided poignant reading at the Remembrance Sunday service in Hemingford Grey in 2016. Bernard Brock Clear had been a young Cambridgeshire village postman and was a larger than life character to his great nephew; his stamp albums, empty but for Victorian definitives, came into my possession as a child and the once occupied spaces held many questions. I knew almost nothing of him, and yet in his 'Soliloquy' was a connection of faith only discovered so many years later.

The urge to find my own expression in words was triggered by profound moments that disturbed my inner being, and the weight of turmoil in the world, provoked me to take up a pencil and search for words.

My earliest recent writing began by responding to the pain we shared with our son and daughter-in-law when their second child, a daughter Zoe, lived for only a few moments. It would be another three years before I took notice and began to write again. Taking the space given by the Covid-19 pandemic for self-isolation and restricted face to face engagement with others, I began to respond on the backs of envelopes.

So I dedicate this book to Bernard and Zoe who lived a century apart but now enjoy the glorious company of the saints. They were the God-given agents who helped me find expression in words that now scan back and forth through my life time, some of which have settled in these pages.

Peter Cunliffe, Spring 2022

A Soliloquy

The North Winds blow – the snow falls fast
To troubled souls, comes the wintry blast
No peace has man, that he calls his own
No peace in nature or by hearth's stone

It's War – and Hell – and Hell's weird cries
Sure leap o'er earth and reach the skies
The roar of cannon, the shriek of shell
The stricken, the wounded, they hear death's knell

England Calls – in voice both loud and clear
From Fen, Hill, Dale – the men are here!
Ready! Aye ready! Sire, son, grey-hair and youth
Fighting for loved ones, fair home and Truth

Its War – War, with its curse and pain
Husband, son, sweetheart! You know not – when again-
With smiles and tears The Story you tell
How you passed to life from Hell

But, the God of Love – who ever knows
Can Peace – Great Peace – bring from your woes
Trust Him – and high above, with splendour bright
Shall shine Heaven's Beacon – Guiding Star of Light

Bernard Brock Clear
Friday 25th February 1916

Zoe Louise Cunliffe

18th May 2017

When my life is only an hour.
What have I to offer?

I was conceived in love.
Love for me grew in your hearts.
I was carried in love.
I was awaited in love.
I was born in pain and left
Tears of pain and broken hearts.
But, my name is life!

It was for life in New Creation
A gift of procreation to my Maker
In whose Book of Life my name,
Zoe Louise, is written.

I leave you behind, my father and mother,
Jono and Kels,
For just the twinkling of the eye
in our eternal home.

In New Creation I will be known
As I am already known
to God my Heavenly Father.

Life in its fullness is the gift
of our good, good Father.
You too can live it now
and we will live it together
as children of God.
Remember, those who live in love,
live in God and God lives in them.

When my life is the gift of God.
I have everything to offer.

Nothing is wasted that God has made.
Zoe Louise

Through the pen and tears of my grandfather

Place

Sitting in Costa in Louth on a rainy day, I was carrying a small notebook and pencil with the intention of using it write down observations, thoughts or notes. I felt ill-equipped to write anything on its pristine pages but the church spire compelled me to begin.

The Spire

The highest in the land
Piercing grey-leaden sky
Drawing down penetrating rain
Reaching the heavens with its praise

Gazing over rolling wolds
Verdant green with watered winter wheat
Joined by a nave of measured-out few
Humming their praise to the forgotten One.

The sign 'Church Open' in front a closed door
but make no mistake, heaven's open to all who call
Stones cry out with nature's praise
This spire of aspiration
Calling out our upward gaze to the One.

Randomly visiting Cleethorpes while spending a few days in Lincolnshire and realising I had visited the seaside from the City of Sheffield as a small child, travelling there by train.

Cleethorpes

A place of distant memory
Seaside as a child
Pier
End of the line railway station
Cod and chips
And then the wakener
Donkey rides on the beach
Sixty years have passed!

North Sea in October

White-crested
in opposition
to flat grey skies

Grief and Loss

Reflecting on the recent death of parishioners while life carries on:

Prayer from a Sorrowful Heart

When the bright autumn sun
fills the golden leaves with light
I see them fall, scattered on the ground.
Those eyes that once delighted in the beauty, now closed
and in my heart a space.

You are the God of the living I know
But tear the veil that separates us from you
No longer to long for the day we see again
The fullest radiance, in the splendour of your being
Find our deepest longings satisfied.

While all creation sings your praise
The weight of sorrow stills my voice
To wait with you.

When a close member of the church family dies making the announcement is personal.

Announcement

One is missing

But none is lost

Sheep in the fold, enfolded

Thinking about separation.

Missing Someone

You created our hearts for fellowship with one another.
Yet in this time the stuttering rhythms of life
have broken the sweetness of simple embrace.
We find ourselves bearing the sorrow of separation.

We acknowledge, O Lord, that it is good and right
to miss deeply those whom we love
but with whom we can not be physically present.
Grant us the courage to love well and wisely during this
    pandemic
and to shrink neither from the aches nor joys that love brings.

So I will choose to praise you even in the midst of sadness,
knowing that all in this life will in your perfect time be
    redeemed.

Having delivered a card to say we remember this day too

The Anniversary of Loss

When I turn the page in my diary, O Lord,
it is heavier than all the others.
I have been feeling the weight
of this page for weeks
and now it is here.

That number marks the day,
the anniversary of my loss,
and its here again like a day of rain
when what I need is a refreshing shower
followed by warm sunshine.

O Lord redeemer, redeem this day.
*I do not ask that these lingerings
of grief be erased**, but that
like a gentle brush through tangled hair
I might feel again the caress of floating locks
and the breath of your Spirit.

You are present, Lord, so speak
in whispered words of grace,
that even as I hear them
the sounds of dawn may also come
as hope of the new world.

As the loss-hallowed day arrives
in all my years to come,
remind me that you set eternity
in every human heart.

May my past wound,
and the memory of it, Lord,
spur me to be closer present with you,
in ways that I was not before,
making me fully alive to the pain and joy,
the sorrow and hope of my life with you.

* A phrase from Douglas Kaine McKelvey, *Every Moment Holy,*
Rabbit Room Press, Nashville, 2017.

The Pandemic

Prayer While Waiting

As my life is lived in anticipation,
this Covid waiting in so so slow.
I can't hold my waiting-breath longer,
I want to let it go
When I breathe in again, can it be
with new life from you, my God?

Forgive my unrighteous impatience,
directed at those who are doing their best
Increase instead my capacity for a righteous grace
and an ability to see that future day
of your return when all creation will be set free.

Be present in this moment,
set it free from all the others, to enjoy
The wonder of my God come near,
waiting with us longing the day
to share heaven's joy, its glory and dazzling light.

I am as fragile as you made me,
my aching heart you know.
Fill me again, with your breathe
of life and grace to wait for you.
(October 2020)

When the daily death toll from Covid-19 in the UK exceeded one thousand

Daily Deaths Peak

The news is bleak as cold this winter's day
Snow is falling and for a moment gives a sense of play
Truth is a somber reality as newscaster recites the daily toll
The rock of life's certainty has become the shifting sand

No longer do we strive oblivious of our temporal frailty
and the invisible threat
Careless of the precious gift of breath and without a thought
Except to turn again in hope that God is listening after all
Light a candle and offer a prayer in churches
that have seen it all before.

Surrounded by fields of winter wheat
sprouting in ice-filled furrows
Vast heaven reaching down to touch our fenland horizon
calling my upward gaze beyond the blue
to the One who sits enthroned in Heaven's glory
Holding in His hand earth-spinning chaos secure

As each day's fight for life concede's to tomorrow's,
wearied carers fall in restless sleep.
But there is hope to see, beyond the mask and goggles,
for those with mustard seeds of faith
Life is more than breath and number of days,
for eternity is planted in the human heart.
So I will not fear that breath will cease.

Seeds sown in icy fen die and rise to life,
Field's furrows now with tiny shoots becoming a sea of green
Nothing separates us from our purpose
nor the One whose eternal name is breath itself.

My soul inspires the vision before my eyes of heaven's glory
Bleak the news may be, but not a single sparrow falls unnoticed
Every detail of God's unfolding plan known to him
with promised transfiguration and new creation.

When Guilt and Grief come together

An explosion of emotion erupts.
What hope is there in being whole again,
Of finding peace with loose ends unfinished?

Pain avoiding, corner fighting.
Peace! What peace? Can yours be real
Amidst the trouble of this fear wielding-virus?

Who gives hope to pain and light to reveal
A door of freedom from the darkness of despair?
Can time replay, to heal our wounds.

There's not a hope in hell - but rumour says,
"Someone will shoulder our pain.
Heaven's where there's such a One."

He took our guilt and bore it on a cross.
Can this be true?
The grief of loss still pains my soul.
"I'll take your heart of stone," he said,
"and give you one of flesh."

The Promise sounds, of hope to come,
Of love to soften and heal
lifts my gaze, beyond myself,
to love and be made whole.

The Shepherd's Crook

While visiting a parishioner in the hospice early in the morning. Amongst other things she was suffering with macular degeneration. I read aloud Psalm 24.

An Hour of Peace

A blanket of grey softness
Muffled stillness enfolding
Through the window light seeping
She lay quiet breathing
Waiting to ascend the hill of the LORD
Your word voiced
Made alive by your Spirit
LORD, let your servant depart in peace
Misty vision clearing
To behold the One
Arms reaching out in welcome
Faithful servant coming
A banquet awaiting
The Master's House

The Wounded Dog Bites.

How sharp are those teeth
It's not that blood was spilled
But that it should think I do not care
When its pain obliterates the truth
And the joy of anticipation lost
The hanging lead knows no sorrow
It awaits the Master's hand
Tomorrow, in radiant light, meadows await
But in this moment I AM here
I hold a morsel in my hand
It is not in our going or in our doing
But in our being your are the Master's best friend.

Taking a graveside funeral service on a bitter winter day.

Sunless Winter Afternoon

Nineteen minutes journey time.
Traffic light leave in ten.
"After three-quarters of a mile turn left"
Wipers intermittent wiping, engine purring, cruising
Snow-covered fields passing, low lit grey skies
Endless trucks trucking.
Hearse linen-casket bearing centenarian.

Pace slowing "exit approaching, turn right on New Road"
Woodland burial ground stretching out over lowland hills
Cold penetrating stitching earth to sky
Cluster upon cluster of mounded graves telling the somber story
of twenty twenty and twenty-one.

We walk ice crunching gravel and out
beyond the hedge on muddied path
Rising hill-ward as buzzard glides on winter winds
a fresh dug heap beckons.
As with steady step the casket is carried to its resting place,
"I am the resurrection and the life", says the Lord.

No final resting place will this be
but the place from which resurrection eyes
Will see tree covered hills matured by years
as the Lord of Glory appears.
Pausing our time to commend the passing loved-one,
whose days are written in God's book,
"Thy kingdom come, thy will be done"
when His face we will see.

Our time is in His hands
and then a timeless day will break
And all our tears accounted for
The Son's light shining in hope-filled hearts.

After a difficult email about a parishioner suffering with cancer

When Tears Well Up

Why? Why? Why? we want to scream
Your mercy hidden by pain
Leafless trees holding the promise of Spring
Defying Winter's chill
This window-framed defiance before my eyes
Powerless words of apology escape
"I'm sorry"
But the powerful words, "It is finished" made all aright

Assisted living is how it is
Breath on breath drawing us nearer
Life of love in fullness finding
Cry of pain labours for life
Giving birth in me

Gripping tightly my Lover's hand
I hold on until mercy reaches and takes my hand
Stepping into warm Spring air
Leaving my pain for others to bear
Until all things and all are made new.

After meeting a mother and child on the doorstep. The child was asking,

---

"Will I know my big sister when we get to heaven?"

Thoughtful eyes looked up
A smile from heaven looked down
Moses and Elijah with Jesus stood
We'll know and be known

Tiny was the coffin laid
But full of stature she will be
When raised to life eternal
A Saviour and a brother meet

What pain our earthbound spirit bears
As on hallowed ground we stand
What hope our souls inspire
As promised life receive

'Twill be a meeting glorious
Clothed in resurrection light
When pain will cease and life begin
Knowing and fully known.

Final Assault on Faithful Love

It came
Cancer the uninvited guest
Pain shouting at the slightest move
With brutal determination she arose
In search of freedom
Quiet click of motor starting
Road rolling

Breath holding until journey's end
Slipping like liquid gold thro' trembling hands
Painful parting
Tears rolling, breath gasping
Quiet click of motor stopping
Emptiness awaiting

Hope still holding for pain control
Battle winning Faithful One weeps
Tomorrow is in His hands.

When Blue Lights Flash

When the flashing of blue lights catch the eye
Hearts miss a beat, a sense of foreboding falls
Leaning towards the window at the chatter of 'copter blades
Wondering who now may be suffering pain
Will the resources to care be sufficient or
Is the brevity of life to be revealed once again.

May the fearful cries of all who bear God's image come to him
And he draw near to them
God, whose compassion took him to a cross
Be merciful in this day-of-the-world's-deep-need
Resurrected One come among us, enfold us with mercy
Breathe your life-breath into weary lungs.

Yahweh, giver of life, give a second-breath
Dispel the shadow of Covid with your healing holy light.
May the joy of loving-life return in the skip
of old and young alike
That, with the majestic cry of all creation,
our lips might find new songs of praise.
Lord, have mercy.

The World

The stories in the weekend press are bleak; exploitation of natural resources, disregard of the natural environment, homelessness, global conflicts and a focus on self.

The News

I stop to listen for the voice of God
  in the stillness of an ending day.
My head ringing with tinnitus, that sound unheard by others
causing me to ponder how silence really sounds
  or if it can be heard at all.

I feel my chest rising and with the air I breathe
  comes the breath of God,
this ruach life, the promise of safe-keeping in a polluted world.

The world wakens or sleeps, though many are sleep less,
their problems a burden too heavy to bear.
With heavy heart I am reminded that these burdens are not
  mine,
the Word told me to bear his yoke and then my burdens would
  be light.

Wild fires rage around the globe,
and fires set by men raze the forest;
torrential rain brings flooding as homes and lives and
livelihoods are swept away;
icecaps fall into oceans and the earth shakes.

Will we allow our insatiable appetite
for news of others' burdens weigh us down,
when loving God and neighbour is all that we are asked?

TV ads tell us to travel where we can,
'green light' permitting of course,
and, that in seeing the world, we will be made whole again!

But when I look, with open eyes, I see 'kings' rise and fall,
trusting in flying horses of steel to no avail;
these no sure defence against unseen principalities and powers.

Of righteous kings and kingdoms there is but One,
His kingdom has come, yet unseen by blinded eyes
we strive to make ourselves the king.

Unexpectedly the righteous king will come in triumph.
Justice and peace will prevail;
the silence of eternity and the constant ringing broken
by songs of everlasting praise.

News of a neurosurgical appointment for my wife, followed by news of 26 migrants drowning in the English Channel.

Winter's Sleep

November morning, 52° north.
A blanket of thick cloud obscures the shining sun;
Gold carpets the ground,
Trees stand proud entering their winter's sleep.

The pace of life marches on relentlessly
Oblivious to the unfolding tragedy on our southern shore of
Dreams evaporating in uncertainty.

The call of freedom allures precious ones to an early icy grave;
Smugglers spend their ill-gotten gains on all that will pass
    away.
The bank of heaven's claim
"None will be lost - not one small lamb" is hard to hear
While sinking in the inky blue, the stars look on
As in their twinkling, souls rest in winter's sleep.

What is the value of politicians words,
Whose mouths well fed and
Bodies warm, as these dear ones face chilling pain?
Nations turn away from jubilees of grace;
Sou'westered crews scan the dark in vain
Hoping the tide of the fearful nationless will turn
And rest will come for all in winter's sleep.

The shattered light of an early winter
Dawn rises over this southern shore
Where stumbling steps, poor, lost and cold,
Crunch this pebbled land,
The sound of sea receding.
A crushing flood of grief and relief in hearts and minds,
And still they come the tide of searchers
For home and a winter's sleep.

Ukraine

Holding hope for a retirement and searching for somewhere to live seems trivial in the context of war and those whose homes and livelihoods have been taken away.

Looking for a Home

Not driven by the guns of war but retirement,
Leaving behind twenty years in a parish, a vicarage that has been home
Searching everyday for somewhere new to start afresh.

The way each day is clouded yet God's provision is the means,
The horizon misted by an old command, to have an open home.
Will unknown neighbours open a door of welcome,
And the family God's people reach out to embrace?

The stuff of life we sort, of which dust will be made.
But letting go and trusting, not in accumulation, but in the One
Who fills every space, whenever invited,
no matter how large or small.

Lifting the cover of her precious white grand piano,
she sits and plays one last time.
Music fills the air while all around the shattered home is strewn
The juxtaposition of peace and violence
is no longer unimaginable in the dust.

Leaving, suspended on one last note,
a house and home to find a way of escape.
As driven by the guns of war the music-maker flees
the noise of war, the shattering blast of missiles.

Leaving behind the place of home and work and worship.
Searching everyday for safety, on the long trek, to rest awhile.
Pressing on to find somewhere to call home,
holding tight their young.
Fleeing west towards the setting sun
and from the black clouds of war.

Will a door of welcome wait the unknown neighbours —
your neighbour who is coming, broken by the pain of loss,
hungry for food and a loving embrace,
afraid of being misunderstood by a cloud of suspicion
but holding the promise of the God of peace
in a pure and endless note?

Lenten reflection. Seeing the colours of the Ukraine flag in my mind with green leaves shooting up between yellow and blue light.

Light

Vibrant yellow and blue makes green.
Liquid blue the cosmic dome.
Growing, nourishing, green of Spring.
Whatever darkness brings,
the light of hope is undiminished in
God's redeeming purpose.

Frail as we are,
the vessels of the Holy One,
bearing in our bodies, heart and mind
the dying pains inflicted by the Evil One,
we hold too the promise
of ruach breath and shekinah glory.

Tears of disbelief all counted,
nothing lost, not one small lamb.
For pierced was the Lamb of God
but bright his resurrection dawn
in which we live forever in his life-giving reign,
the waters of life flowing between the green.

Reflecting on reports of a Russian advance on Kyiv and the plight of those seeking refuge.

Seeking Refuge

Pressing through the bureaucratic night
Ground shaking under wave of obliteration
Driven by survival, mother and child flee
Longing for a place of peace and security
Overwhelming silence from a husband and son
Seeking welcome and life again.

The future holds no temporal promise of joy
Gathered around the family table
Or of kneeling to receive the host of heaven,
But the Kyrie cry reaches our eternal home
Whose open door is the saviour king.

Dreams evaporated in the missile blast
Icy winds blowing the dust of war
Towns and cities, once vibrant, lay in desolation
Silenced now but holding in their memory
A husband and a son who stood, to defend
A right to live and love in peace.

Heavy is the unknowing future on a mother's heart
Sacrificial lambs both slaughter and are slaughtered
Premature the exchange, mortal for immortality,
or eternal death.

No escape from hell on earth but through a rugged cross
Disturbed, unsettled, though holding
victory in the midst of misery,
Waiting the dawn of heaven's eternal day.

Creation

Sunrise

The air is cold
Stillness settled fields
Birds stirring
Signs of life
Golden hour
Eastern horizon
Red fractured clouds shot through
Dark clouds giving way to colour
Sunrise
Each day's advent
Divine promise
Of a New Day Coming

Dawn

The promise of a new day
Sunlight-fractured cloud
Recapturing colour from monochrome
Retreating night
Heart awakening hope
The return of farther vision
Sun rising

Underneath are the Everlasting Arms
Bearing in His hands the whole world
Son-fractured death gives way to life
Redeeming dazzling beauty
Truth declaring greater reality
Eternity set in every human heart
End of ends
A new beginning

I Thought the Day Was Ending

Forbidding clouds of night
Pushing back the brightness of the day
Deep shadows threaten
Father, do you really love me?

I'm counting my years
Constraining finite possibilities
Holding seeds of hope I come
Seeking new horizons

The promise of a new day coming
Light dawning from forgiveness
Given and received
In the radiance of your glory
I choose to walk by faith

Time

My wife has a vestibular schwannoma and it's another month before surgery.

Waiting

Waiting for the known and the unknown
The revealed and the hidden
This tension of faith stretched to an imagination of
The promised life to come.

Waiting in the dusty reality of an ageing earth
Marred by misadventure and lust for treasure
The daily spark, so easily dulled to smouldering smoke
Is cupped by the hand and breath of Light.

Waiting and wondering what a new day will bring
As advancing in silent space a lesion grows unopposed
The viral crisis restraining helping hands
Trusting in Sovereign purposes and the coming new creation

Waiting for centuries in silent anticipation as
He watches over his people, what are four weeks to
The promise-maker and -keeper who holds eternity
In his hand and hides it in the human heart.

Waiting for that day when disappointment, grief and fear is gone
Each breath a gift and each heart beat of body and soul
A knowing-the-indwelling-One whose heart holds
In love the Crown of Creation.

Kicking heels

The wisdom of unhurried grace persists
I look around searching for space fillers
As if I alone can redeem the waiting time
The hour-hand's rotation constraining possibilities, and yet
With God all things are possible, unlimited, unconstrained.

Once again creative imagination, dexterity and provision
Join together to reveal, in the ordinary, the transcendent
Work is done with time to rest a moment along the way.
My carefully planned diary leaves but little time for space
Yet the overruling One brings about his purposes of peace.

If only I would live in the freedom of Christ's example
To be waylaid, held back, but only in the eyes of time.
When trusting in his faithfulness, experience confirms
A greater dimension on which edge I tread,
God's purpose to do the unexpected, unplanned for extra mile
the seed for fruit in due season.

When the Sun Rises Late and Sets Early

When gentle shadows of night
Cover us with God's peace
For a little while we spin
In light of moon and stars
While all around the earth
Is cradled in the sun's embrace.

I gaze out into deepest blue
Under the all-seeing eye of One
Whose name is breath
And feel the lift of angels wings
As Heaven's Armies' flight
Watches o'er the Sons of God.

When morning breaks and I awake
Rested and renewed I stand
Strong in the Son's light
While all around the earth is held
In the Father's hand.

Delight

Feeling the weight of recent deaths in the parish and deciding to look for joy, beyond the sadness, in the things around:

Finding Joy

Clouds skipping in blue skies

Sunlight dancing on leaves

Squirrels chasing

Workmen singing

Baby talking

Skipping

A tiny living thing on the hand of a child

A first smile

A postcard

Listening

The wind rustles leaves
a bee buzzes
a motorbike splutters and booms
a car sings
a helicopter chatters
youthful voices
the crack of pigeon wings
a small aeroplane hums
and the wheels of a trolley rattle.

For a moment the sounds of peace,
a bird sings and rustling leaves return.
What is man that you are mindful of him?

A Wedding

Menorah light illuminated the west window
Winter sun splashed cooler on *St James' White* walls
A small circle of chairs filled the chancel
A pair of doves lighting from the sanctuary kneeler.

Family gathered in a chatter,
brother is best man, sister maid of honour,
nephew scattered petals and niece wanted Daddy.
Grandma beamed as kilt-clad father-of-the-bride
Walked his daughter down the aisle.
Slender gold rings slid and danced on ancient stone
Soon placed securely on young hands.

An invocation of blessing over the happy couple, before
Scripture and poetry read, the Wedding at Cana revisited.
Prayers lifted to the throne of heaven and
all received God's blessings.

Two families united as one,
bells pealed out over river and meadow,
the Winter sun's waning light
warming 11th century walls with golden beam.

Words written in a Birthday Card

Bright sun
Last of autumn gold
Jewels of frost
Sparkling drops
Verdant green
Dazzling blue
Advent for a birthday

Life

Christmas at St James' Church, Hemingford Grey, standing by the river Great Ouse in Cambridgeshire and over looking river meadows.

Christmas Eve 2020

Yesterday at church:
Heavy laden skies
Pressing greyness against 11th century walls
Windows bejewelled with dancing flame
Cold seeping, warm praise rising
Voices raised
"Come, O long expected Jesus"
River swirling, prayers rising,
Rain competing,
"He is the King of Glory"

Today
Skies blue of heaven
Lifting souls with promise,
Hope arising
The King is coming,
Knees bow,
Hearts sing
"Come, O long expected Jesus
Born to set your people free
From our fears and sins release us
Let us find our rest in you."

Tomorrow

Immanuel's birthday
Births birthdays
For all in whom Christ is born.
Spirit filling softened hearts
Spilling Christmas praise.
Jesus fire within us
Send your glory,
Salvation for our world.

After watching a Great Tit visiting the nest box outside my study window.

Fledgling Photographer

Armed with a full-frame sensor and an eye for light
The last of our brood took wing
Encircling the globe taking landfall in warmer climes
Finding there the delight of his eye
to call home the Pacific shore.

Trailing from the nest box evidence of its occupancy.
Personal belongings now packed and sent.
Soon Spring beckons another visitor and so the cycle continues.
Fresh materials sought; methodical nest building
The response to the Maker's design
a little home on a Pacific shore.

Days of frantic feeding from bugs hanging on threads.
Cries of "da-da" draw his enfolding wing
Soon the summer's leaves call for more careful observation
The little brood takes uneasy wing or tottering steps
as the school of life beckons fledgling and infant.

Armed with a full-frame sensor and an eye for light
The last of our brood took wing
Encircling the globe taking landfall in warmer climes
Finding there the delight of his eye
to call home the Pacific shore.

Remembering my work as a paediatric nurse in PICU, the births
of several babies close to my heart and their parents.

Newborn

Breathless from the womb you came
Surrounded by the machinery of resuscitation

Deft hands brought the the first cool breaths
Till crying out you gasped for air

Tiny but imperfectly formed fragile child
So full of potential and sunny days
Laying in the palm of my hands
Soft touch of warm skin and infant breath

Cocooned in radiant heat, separated from mother's beating heart
I whisper cooing sounds to listening ears
Turning the helpless body of this precious soul
Her bright eyes searching

Tiny fingers move to grasp with featherlike caress
Heart beat, racing to a dancing trace, calmed by a loving stroke
How soon the wide-world will open out
But for now a mother's gift is out of reach, the bliss of breast
denied.

A prayer before the surgeon's skill reunites disconnected parts,
Adding alien tubes and wires.
Father reaches hesitatingly to touch his gift,
Mother lies asleep on the edge of life.

This cocktail of pain and joy falls heavy on young shoulders,
Tears fall for lost dreams and relief and joy.
Years of watchfulness await the journey of healing,
In this moment a fearful uncertainty of anxious waiting.

Father holds in his heart the newborn's name
Until his wife awakens from her sleep
Battle-scarred, clawed back from the edge of life
With weakened voice she speaks her name.

It was the birth day of a grandson and having often wondered
what it was like on the day I was born I sat to record the day
that had just been so that he might share it.

The Nineteenth of November

In nautical twilight you came   —the advent of the day

Before a glorious golden hour of sunrise —the promise

The air was crisp   —alive

The last of autumn's golden leaves   —the season's cycle

A light drizzle   —life in rain

Day ending with a dazzling sunset   —rest is coming

Soft shadows falling with the night   —enfolding grace

A waxing crescent moon in misty sky —light in the darkness

Your birthday, Rupert Douglas   —a gift.

Thanks be to God.

When Sunday worship could not be held in person we gathered with our mission partners from around the world, on Zoom.

First Sunday of Advent

An unassuming grey day

Pastries proved, oven hot

Coffee poured

Zoom-gathering chatter

Spanning half a globe

Candle lit

Voices raised

O Come, O Come Emmanuel

When going for a retinal scan

Routine Appointment

Today I had a driver take me
Guided to a covid-safe venue.
Eye drops stung and pupils dilated
Clouds awesome grey through tinted office windows.

Waiting room stories from a world away
Of summer sun and sizzling heat
A lockdown torment of another Kiwi reality
Or optimism for summer to come?

"Rest your chin, follow the light light", clunk and flash
"You'll get the report, see you in a year."
Guided out into cold air swirling with snow
Departing, blurred vision, home bound.
Such confidence in a year to come
Was it blurried faith or blind?

While I pause and wait, vision sharpening
I see with sight again
Focussed on the here and now
But looking to a future horizon
Of departures and arrivals
to bless and be blessed.

Seasons

Winter Trees

Sun piercing

Morning's mist parting

Light caught in Spring-waiting trees

Reaching for azure blue

The promise of sap rising

Bejewelled with sparkling drops

Spiny branches dressed

Lichen verdant rich

Alder cones dripping liquid amber

Silver birch in golden bloom

Showering ardent rain

How can I stop with so much to do?

Sovereign Lord, my list of to-do's is so demanding
But you demand nothing.
Your hands reach out with gifts of grace
And offer peace which makes the impossible possible.

When the voices of creation disturb my thoughts as noise
I focus again remembering that the creature's voice is its praise
Held in time with the silent music of creation.
As I listen to this silent music embracing your still small voice
I listen and hear the whisper of my name

Summer's trees stretch in magnificence towards the heavens
Leaves if every hue shimmer in the breeze.
Splashes of colour in the green grass dance over a microcosm
Too small for the passing eye to see
Where insects go about their work
In obedience to the Creator's grand design.

As clouds part to reveal the universal blue
I am awoken from my contemplation to give my praise
To the One who bids me rest
To lay down my list and sleep.

The Vineyard

Swiss precision blade sprung from its anvil
in the vine dresser's hand.
Crisp the air and pure white the frost covering the vine,
he reached the canes,
A perfect embrace of stillness in a restless world.
The winter vine standing leafless, sap no longer flowing,
This purposeful cutting back looks forward
to another season's fruit.

Deft mind unconsciously counting buds as sparks fly upward.
Fire dancing in the cold air warms his face, as fed by handful
Of slender canes, their fruit long gathered in.
Tangled vine-wood reduced to trunk and arms,
Living words resounding,
"I AM the vine, you are the branches."

Sky turns grey as the blue fades,
Bird song quiets, a hush descends,
Snowflakes in flurries settling on hardened earth
Crushed under foot.
Smoke curls from the vineyard hut
While inside woven wicker baskets wait
Another year, and an empty bottle gathering dust,

Cast aside in carefree summer play through dappled sunlit alleyways.

Closing the latch, the vine dresser kicks off his boots.
Racing thoughts of spring, summer and then autumn harvest
Turn to this years's vintage and the joy it will bring.
Christ in me the hope of glory in years to come, branches pruned
And seasons pass, sparks fly upward and souls are gathered in.

New Wine of God's Kingdom come.

Winter

It's grey again, the sky
weighing down, horizon constraining
a wintry stillness holding
back a breakthrough of snow.

For a moment an uplifting flash
of bird wings breaks through
the deadness of the failing light and
catkins shimmer in their passing wake.

Nothing moves in the dusky twilight
as the mercury falls, except the cat
stretching from its daytime slumber.
Thoughts of distant warm, sunny days
awakened in my sleepy head.

The rhythms of the seasons embracing
the longer imperceptible cycles of life
advancing, counting down my finite
days which only yesterday seemed infinite.

The street light, which once began to glow
is now instantly on, pouring its pool
of growing light into the street.

Darkened trees merge with a starless sky, a new nocturne.
The deep blue of night is pierced by lamp lights,
Gentle breeze holding the promise of celestial breakthrough
adds hope to a new day's dawn heralded by the morning star.

After cancelling the visit of my father for Christmas and packing gifts in a bag. The following should be read with a West Riding Yorkshire accent.

Christmas in a Bag

Lunch will come as it usually does
with a ring on the door at twelve.
Today it will be turkey roast and steamed Christmas pud.
Carols from Kings I'll be playing and,
after the cheery greeting at the door,
I'll be alone with my thoughts, but…I have Christmas in a bag.

A small living tree with a robin bedecked
and an aroma of English cheese.
There's a pot of No.1 New Zealand honey,
some English marmalade,
and what feels like a bar of chocolate wrapped up in stars.

Covid holds back my children, grandchildren and great, but
soon my iPad pings with pictures and Skype calls,
we chat for a bit but…at least I have Christmas in a bag.

I'll pull the cracker, put on their silly hat,
laugh at that 100-year-old-joke —
long enough to stop for a handful of mixed fruit and nuts.
At three I turn on the TV while that peer of mine
gives her Christmas speech.
I bet she's not got…Christmas in a bag.

Endnote

Rediscovered while compiling this book. Written by a parishioner sixteen years ago as she reflected on the humanity of her Parish Priest soon after the death of one of the Churchwardens.

For Peter

If we put you on a pedestal
And do not let you be human,
We have failed to love.

If we think that pain will skirt round you
And your calling will shield you,
We have failed to love.

If we expect you to carry on regardless,
To bury the pain to meet another obligation,
We have failed to love.

So we commit you to the Father,
Whose love gave us Emmanuel
To share every human experience
And show us the face of God;

To the Son,
Whose feet got tired and mucky,
Who was so weary he slept in a boat through a storm,
Who wept at the death of a friend;

To the Spirit,
Who walks beside us,
Whose gentle breath sings joy into pain,
Who reminds us of the many mansions
of the Father's house,

To Alpha and Omega, the Beginning and the End,
To Tony's God and ours,
In whom is no withdrawing of presence,
No absence of grace,
No failure to love,
Throughout time and for eternity, Amen

Judith Hall, Trinity Sunday 2006